AF488293

FROM HERE TO HERE

365 MOMENTS OF CLARITY

EKL

Copyright © 2025 by EKL
First Edition

All rights reserved.
No part of this book may be used or reproduced in any
manner whatsoever without written permission.

Cover & layout by Max Lollar

ISBN: 979-8-9936433-0-4

FROM

HERE

TO

HERE

This book is not a doctrine, but a doorway. The 365 Lessons of From Here to Here are daily reflections designed to gently loosen the grip of separation, fear, and striving by inviting you back - again and again - into the quiet truth of who and what you truly are. Each day offers a simple yet profound reminder, a still point around which the noise of the world can settle. These lessons are rooted in the timeless insights of nonduality, quantum awareness, and mystical wisdom drawn from East and West alike.

You will find that certain truths repeat, sometimes subtly, sometimes clearly. This is intentional. The mind is conditioned through years of repetition - through habits of thought, identity, and reaction. To awaken from these habits requires not complexity, but gentle persistence. Repetition is not redundancy, it is reinforcement. A single drop of truth may ripple through your day, but layered drops shape the contours of a new way of seeing. Allow these lessons to be companions rather than concepts. Let them be read, re-read, and lived. Some days they may land in the mind; other days, they may settle in the heart. Trust that both are part of the unfolding. And most of all, trust that the peace you seek is already present, quietly waiting to be noticed.

Take your time remembering this knowledge –

Sip, don't gulp.

Welcome home.

You Are Not the Wave, You Are the Ocean

Your identity is not limited to your body, thoughts, or roles. Like a wave that rises and falls, you appear to be separated - but your true nature is the boundless ocean of awareness.

The World You See Is a Mirror

What you perceive in others reflects what lives in you. See beauty, and beauty is yours. See conflict and ask what is unresolved within. The world reflects your consciousness.

Stillness Is Your Natural State

Beneath the movements of thought and emotion is a profound stillness. It is always present, never disturbed. Rest there. It is your true home.

Love Is What You Are

Love is not something you give or get - it is the radiance of your being. When all defenses fall away, what remains is love.

You Do Not Think - Thinking Happens

Thoughts arise in awareness, like clouds drifting across the sky. You are not the thinker; you are the sky that holds all weather.

The Present Moment Is the Only Reality

Past and future exist only in thought. Now is where life happens, where truth lives. Return to it again, and again.

Suffering Is Resistance to What Is

Pain arises in life, but suffering is the mind's refusal to allow it. When you stop resisting, peace returns.

You Are Not the Body

The body changes. It ages, feels, responds.
But you - the one aware of the body - are
changeless. Discover that witness.

Everything Is an Expression of the One

Nothing is outside of the whole. Each thing, each being, is a unique wave arising from the same ocean. See the unity behind all forms.

There Is No Other

Separation is an illusion born of thought. Look deeper and you will find that there is no "other" - only One, appearing as many.

Awareness Is Always Here

No matter the chaos, no matter the change - awareness never leaves. It is the unmoved witness, always present. Rest in it.

Let Go of the Story

You are not your history. You are not the
narrative that plays in your mind. You are
the silence in which the story arises -
and dissolves.

Peace Cannot Be Found, Only Realized

You cannot chase peace. You can only stop running from it. It is not something to gain, but something to uncover.

Trust the Space Between Thoughts

In the gap between thoughts is truth. Do not fear the silence - it holds more wisdom than any word. Listen there.

You Belong to the Whole

There is nothing in you that is separate from the All. You are a thread in the sacred fabric of existence. You are already included.

There Is No Path, Only Uncovering

Enlightenment is not about building - it's about removing what never was. You are not becoming - you are revealing.

The Mind Is a Faithful Servant, a Poor Master

Let the mind serve the heart. Let thought arise from presence. But do not bow to it - it cannot lead you home.

The Heart Recognizes Truth Instantly

You do not need to analyze what is true. The heart knows before the mind catches up. Trust its quiet clarity.

Nothing Real Can Be Threatened

Your essence is untouchable. It cannot be wounded or diminished. Know what you are, and fear dissolves.

Let Everything Be as It Is

Peace is not found in controlling life, but in allowing it. When you stop resisting, grace enters.

You Are Already Whole

No achievement will complete you. No future moment will deliver you. Wholeness is now, because you are That.

Freedom Is Found in Surrender

True freedom comes not from control, but from letting go. Surrender reveals the vastness you already are.

You Are the Awareness Behind the Eyes

The one who sees is not your name, age, or history. You are the seeing itself. Pure, boundless, and free.

Let the Ego Be Transparent

You need not destroy the ego. Simply see through it. Let it be translucent, and its weight vanishes.

There Is Nothing Outside of Consciousness

Everything known, seen, felt - all of it appears in you. The world does not arise from matter, but from mind.

Love Needs No Object

Love is not a transaction. It does not require an object. It radiates naturally when you are aligned with your true nature.

You Are the Space,
Not the Furniture

Thoughts, emotions, experiences - they come and go like furniture in a room. But you are the space itself: open, untouched, free.

Enlightenment Is the End of the Seeker

When there is no longer a desire to become something else, what remains is truth. The seeker dissolves into the sought.

Let Silence Be Your Teacher

Words can point, but silence reveals. Rest in silence, not as absence, but as sacred fullness.

All Is Well, Even When It Appears Otherwise

Reality is not chaos. Beneath the appearances, there is order, flow, and grace. Trust the deeper rhythm.

You Are the Light
You Seek

Stop looking outside. What you yearn for
is already within you. Let the outer become
quiet, and the inner will shine.

You Can't Lose What You Truly Are

All loss is of form, not essence. What you
are cannot be lost. It simply is. Eternal,
untouched, here.

Allow Rather Than Control

Spiritual growth does not come by force. It comes through allowing. Let what is be. And in that space, all unfolds.

Return Again and Again to the Now

You will forget. That's okay. Simply return.
Each day is a new invitation to practice
resting in the present moment.

This Is It

Not later. Not after awakening. This. This breath, this feeling, this moment. It is whole. It is sacred. It is enough.

Gratitude Aligns You with Truth

Gratitude is not merely polite acknowledgment - it is a recognition of the miracle of being. When you live from gratitude, you attune to the abundance that is always present. Gratitude shifts perception from lack to wholeness, from complaint to communion.

All Beings Are Portals
to the Infinite

Every person you meet holds a gateway to the divine. When you relate to others as the Self in form, your relationships become sacred. The spiritual path is not separate from daily encounters - it is fulfilled through them.

The Universe Reflects Your Inner State

The outer world is a projection screen of your inner vibration. What you believe, fear, or expect tends to shape your experience. Change begins not with fixing the world, but by quieting the mind and realigning your inner frequency to peace.

Spiritual Growth Is Unlearning

You are not here to accumulate more beliefs, but to shed what is untrue. The process of awakening is one of subtraction, not addition. Like a sculptor revealing the form within stone, remove all that you are not, and your essence shines.

Do Nothing,
and All Is Done

In deep alignment, life unfolds effortlessly.
This is the meaning of wu wei - action
through non-action. When the ego gets out
of the way, divine intelligence takes over. You
become the instrument, not the player.

All Forms Are Temporary, But the Essence Is Eternal

The body, thoughts, emotions, relationships - all are forms destined to change. But their essence is timeless. Do not confuse the clay with the pot. Look beyond appearances, and you will find the eternal in everything.

Awakening Is Remembering, Not Attaining

You are not becoming enlightened - you are remembering what you have always been. The journey is not toward something new, but back to something ancient and ever-present. In the stillness of remembering, you return home to the Self.

Non-Attachment Is Supreme Compassion

To love deeply does not require clinging. In fact, non-attachment allows love to breathe and be free. When you no longer seek to possess or control, your presence becomes healing. You give space for others to be, and in that space, love flourishes.

The World Is Not Against You

Life is not happening to you, but through you. What appears as resistance is often grace in disguise. When you stop fighting reality and begin to trust its unfolding, you find an invisible intelligence guiding all things toward awakening.

The Sacred Is Found in the Ordinary

You need not climb mountains or enter caves to discover truth. It reveals itself in dishes washed with attention, in the silence between breaths, in the gaze of a stranger. When the heart is open, the ordinary becomes radiant with the divine.

Stillness Speaks Louder Than Words

In stillness, truth is heard. Beyond the mind's noise, wisdom whispers. When you stop trying to speak, explain, or fix, you become receptive to what is. In the pause between thoughts, the voice of the Self emerges - not loud, but clear.

You Are Not Your History

Your past does not define your essence.
Memory is only a record of the mind,
not a measure of the Self. Who you are is
untouched by all experience. You are the
presence in which every moment has come
and gone. Let the past dissolve in presence.

Life Itself Is Your Guru

Every person, every moment, every emotion is your teacher. There is no need to seek elsewhere. Life brings exactly what is required for your growth - sometimes gently, sometimes fiercely. Meet it all as instruction in the art of being.

Nothing Belongs to You

Not your body, not your thoughts, not even your life is truly yours. Everything is on loan from the universe, passing through. When you relinquish the illusion of ownership, you walk lighter, freer, and more connected to the whole.

Let Go, and the Truth Remains

Truth is not something added but revealed when illusion is removed. You do not need to become more - only less encumbered by false identity. Let go of every mask, and what remains is simple, silent, and eternal: the Self.

The Light You Seek
Is Within

You are not a seeker searching for light - you
are the light through which seeking happens.
When the mind quiets, even briefly, this light
is glimpsed. It was never lost, only obscured
by thought. Rest in your radiance.

Be the Witness, Not the Story

Stories rise and fall in the mind, but the witness remains unchanged. You are not the plot twists, the triumphs, or the tragedies. You are the silent awareness watching the entire play unfold. Identify with that, and suffering softens.

Presence Heals

There is healing in simply being fully present. No need to analyze, explain, or change. Presence itself has a frequency that dissolves tension, fear, and illusion. Be where you are, completely, and transformation begins.

Desire Diminishes in the Light of Being

Desire arises from the illusion that something is missing. But in the fullness of Being, nothing is lacking. As you abide more in your natural state, desire fades - not from suppression, but from fulfillment.

You Cannot Fall Out of the Self

No mistake, no moment of forgetfulness, can remove you from what you are. You may dream of separation, but even the dream happens within the Self. You are always held, even in your forgetfulness.

Understanding Is Not Necessary for Awakening

Intellect can grasp concepts, but awakening is beyond understanding. It is a shift in identity, not a gain in knowledge. Many who know little about theory live in peace. The heart knows what the mind cannot grasp.

The Now Is Not in Time

The present is not a fleeting second between past and future. It is timeless awareness, untouched by chronology. Step out of psychological time and into the now, and you step into eternity.

Let Life Live Through You

You are not the manager of existence. Life breathes, moves, and expresses through your form. When you stop interfering, grace flows. Trust the unfolding and let life be what it is.

Nothing Needs
to Be Fixed

The impulse to fix comes from the belief that
something is wrong. But what if everything
is already whole, already unfolding perfectly?
Relax into what is. Healing begins when you
stop resisting the moment.

Stillness Is the Ultimate Practice

You do not need to master techniques or rituals. Stillness itself is the teaching. Sit, breathe, and be. In that simple stillness, all falsehoods fall away and only truth remains.

The Path Is Made of Your Steps

There is no pre-made road to awakening. Each step you take in awareness lays the path beneath your feet. Don't look for a map - listen inward. The journey is not about where you go, but how deeply you walk.

Rest Is a Sacred Act

Rest is not laziness. It is the return to source, a pause that refreshes your alignment. In rest, the nervous system unwinds, the mind settles, and the heart remembers. Give yourself permission to stop, and healing arises.

All Perception Is Filtered by Belief

What you believe acts like a lens coloring your entire world. Want to see peace? Begin by questioning every belief that disturbs it. As beliefs dissolve, clarity dawns. The world you see changes with the mind that sees it.

The Sacred Cannot Be Owned or Claimed

Truth cannot be branded, bought, or monopolized. It belongs to no religion, culture, or language. The sacred is available to all because it is who we are. It whispers in every heart, regardless of form.

The End of Seeking Is the Beginning of Being

As long as you search, you affirm the illusion that truth is elsewhere. At some point, the search exhausts itself. In that quiet surrender, being reveals itself - not as an answer, but as presence. Stop running, and you arrive.

Emptiness Is Full of Peace

The mind fears emptiness, thinking it means absence or loss. But in spiritual emptiness, nothing is missing. It is the spaciousness that holds all things, the silent peace before the world begins. Dwell there and know contentment.

There Is Nowhere to Get To

Every idea of a better future keeps you one step removed from the truth. You don't awaken by progressing, but by stopping. Right where you are is the doorway. Step into presence, and you are home.

All That Arises Will Pass

Whether joy or sorrow, thought or sensation, everything that appears will dissolve. This is not cause for despair, but freedom. Don't cling to passing waves - rest in the ocean that remains.

Inner Peace Is the Highest Success

True success is not measured by achievement, but by how deeply you abide in peace. When inner harmony becomes your compass, even setbacks become sacred. Success without peace is empty; peace is always a success.

You Are Already That Which You Long For

The longing for truth, love, or God is the call of your own essence. What you seek is not outside you - it is what you are. You long for yourself. Recognize this, and seeking dissolves in fulfillment.

Nothing Is Ever Missing

What appears as lack is often the mind's failure to see the whole. In truth, nothing essential can be missing. Every moment contains precisely what is needed for awakening. Look deeply, and what you thought was absence becomes invitation.

Truth Does Not Argue

Truth is not in competition. It does not need to defend itself or convert others. It simply is. The more aligned you are with truth, the less you need to persuade. Your peace becomes your presence, and your presence speaks louder than words.

Silence Is a Complete Teaching

Silence is not emptiness—it is fullness beyond sound. The highest teaching is given in silence. In silence, there is no distortion, no confusion. What cannot be spoken can be known.

You Are Not a Role, Title, or Identity

All identities are garments the Self wears briefly. They are useful in the world, but not ultimately real. Do not mistake the costume for the actor. You are not the mask - you are the space behind the eyes.

Be Willing to Not-Know

Certainty is often the ego's mask for control. Real wisdom begins with humility - the willingness to dwell in the unknown. In that space of surrender, the mystery becomes a living teacher, and the heart is opened to wonder.

Life Unfolds in Perfect Timing

Impatience arises from the mind; trust comes from the heart. The universe moves with flawless intelligence, even when you do not understand. When you surrender your timeline, you begin to see the grace in delay.

The Self Is Never in Danger

Fear assumes you can be harmed or destroyed. But your true nature is beyond reach. Fire cannot burn it, time cannot age it, words cannot stain it. To realize the Self is to discover invincibility - not of the body, but of being.

What You Accept, Transforms

Judgment locks pain in place. Acceptance dissolves it. When you welcome even your discomfort as a visitor, its grip loosens. The act of allowing is itself the beginning of freedom.

Comparison Is the Thief of Presence

When you compare, you lose touch with what is. The moment becomes clouded by measurement. Return to now. You cannot compare what is with what isn't. Presence is incomparable.

Grace Is Always Available

Grace is not something earned - it is something recognized. It flows continuously, like sunlight, waiting only for you to open the window. When the heart is soft and the mind is still, grace is seen everywhere.

Don't Try to Awaken, Just Be Aware

Effort to awaken implies you are separate from awareness. But you are already awareness itself. Drop the effort. Simply notice. The truth is always present - it only asks to be seen.

Love Without Condition Is Your Nature

The love that expects nothing, needs nothing, and holds no one captive is the love of your true self. It does not change with moods or circumstances. This love flows naturally when ego steps aside.

Resistance Strengthens Illusion

What you resist gains power. The more you fight a thought, emotion, or condition, the more it controls you. But when you allow it to be seen in awareness, it dissolves. Shine the light of presence on it, and watch it fade.

Simplicity Reveals the Sacred

Truth is not complicated. The more you simplify, the more clearly you see. Complexity belongs to the mind. The heart sees directly and with grace. Let go of the extra, and what remains is essence.

There Is No Other

Separation is the root illusion. In truth, there is only one Self appearing as many forms. Every face is your own. Every encounter is a mirror. When you know this, love becomes the only response.

Healing Is Remembering Wholeness

Healing is not about fixing a broken part but seeing that wholeness was never lost. Illness, trauma, confusion - they arise, but they do not touch the core of your being. Return to that core, and healing unfolds.

The Present Is Enough

You don't need a better moment. This one, just as it is, holds all the ingredients of awakening. It may not be what the mind wants, but it is what the soul requires. Be here. This is the doorway.

Rest in the Heart, Not the Head

The mind calculates; the heart knows. The mind worries; the heart trusts. To rest in the heart is to dwell in peace. You do not need to solve life - you only need to feel its pulse within you.

The Divine Is Not Elsewhere

The sacred is not hidden in some distant place. It is woven into every leaf, breath, and gesture. Look closely at the ordinary, and you will see the extraordinary. The Divine is always here.

You Are Already Home

The search ends not in finding, but in realizing you never left. The sense of being lost is part of the play of forgetting. But you cannot leave what you are. You are the Self. You are home.

Everything You Need Is Within You

The wisdom, love, and clarity you seek are already inside you. External teachers and teachings are only mirrors pointing you inward. When you stop looking outside and turn within, the truth is revealed.

Conscious Suffering Burns the Ego

When pain is met consciously, without resistance or story, it transforms. It becomes a fire that purifies, not punishes. The ego withers in this fire, and what remains is clarity and peace. Suffering can be Grace in disguise.

The Self Is Prior
to Thought

Before any idea arises, there is awareness.
That is who you are. You are not your
thoughts, but the space in which they come
and go. Return repeatedly to this space.
It is your home.

The End of Judgment Is the Beginning of Love

Judgment blocks the heart. It creates division and separation. When you suspend judgment - even briefly - love rushes in. Not personal love, but universal love: unconditional, all-embracing, and free.

Let Experience Flow Through You

You do not need to hold on to any moment. Life flows like a river, and your suffering begins when you try to dam it. Allow joy, sorrow, anger, and delight to pass through you. Let it all move and remain the witness.

You Are Already Free

Freedom is not something to attain - it is what you are. The chains are imagined. The door was never locked. When you realize you are the space, not the prisoner, all boundaries dissolve.

Trust Is the Bridge to Peace

Trust life. Trust the intelligence that spins the planets and beats your heart. Even when you do not understand, you can rest in the knowing that something greater holds you. Trust replaces fear with grace.

The Soul Speaks
in Silence

Your deepest wisdom does not come through noise or pressure. It arises in stillness. Be quiet. Listen with your whole being. The answers you seek are already forming like dew in the silence of your heart.

You Are the Mirror and the Reflection

Everything you encounter is a reflection of your inner world. But you are also the mirror—the awareness in which the reflection appears. This double vision brings freedom: you are both the dreamer and the dream.

There Is Only Now

Past and future exist only in thought. Now is the only reality. Whatever peace, love, or presence you long for must be found here. This moment is the doorway to eternity. Step through it.

Reality Is Effortless

The mind believes truth must be hard to find. But reality is the effortless background of all effort. It is the stillness behind every movement. Stop striving, and you will find what you have never left.

Let Love Be
Your Default

When the mind is quiet, love arises naturally. It does not need to be summoned or earned. It is the default state of the open heart. When in doubt, return to love - it is the most direct path to peace.

Awareness Has No Edges

You cannot find a border to awareness. It is boundless, infinite, spacious. Every attempt to locate it reveals its vastness. You are not a point within awareness - you are awareness itself, without limit.

All Seeking Points Back to the Self

Whether seeking success, relationship, peace, or truth, the search always originates in the Self and ends there. You may chase many things, but fulfillment arrives only when you return to who you are.

Pain Is a Messenger, Not an Enemy

Pain signals where love and awareness are being called. It is not a punishment, but a pointer. When met with curiosity instead of resistance, pain becomes a teacher, revealing where healing is needed.

Everything Is Temporary, Except Awareness

All experiences, states, and identities change. But one thing does not: awareness itself. That which watches joy and sorrow is untouched by both. Rest in the changeless, and the changing loses its grip.

The Heart Knows the Way

The intellect hesitates, doubts, and calculates. The heart simply knows. When faced with uncertainty, drop from the head into the heart. Let intuition, not logic alone, guide your steps.

Let It Be Simple

The truth is not complex. The mind complicates, spiritualizes, and analyzes. But awakening is simple: be still, be present, be aware. Let go of the extra, and what remains is peace.

You Are Not Here to Be Perfect

Perfection is a concept, not a truth. You are here to be real, not flawless. Your humanity is not a flaw in the design - it is part of the sacred unfolding. Embrace your imperfections as part of the path.

Don't Take the Mind Personally

Thoughts arise, play out, and dissolve - but they are not you. The mind generates noise, but awareness remains untouched. You are not the one who thinks - you are the one witnessing thoughts arise and fall away.

Being Is Enough

You do not need to prove, improve, or justify your existence. Your very being is already complete. In a world obsessed with doing, remember the power and peace of simply being.

Let Go of the Story

The mind loves to narrate. But peace is not found in the story - it is found in the silence beneath it. When you drop the tale of "me," you fall into presence, where only this moment lives.

Oneness Is Not a Concept, but a Reality

You don't become one with all - you realize you always were. This is not a belief to adopt, but a truth to experience. When the illusion of separation dissolves, only unity remains.

You Are the Witness of Change

Everything around you shifts - emotions, relationships, the body. But there is something that never changes: the one who sees. Identify with the witness, not the waves, and you find inner stability.

Rest Is a Form of Worship

In rest, you honor the sacredness of being. You step out of striving and return to wholeness. Rest renews, re-centers, and reconnects. To rest deeply is to remember your true nature.

Surrender Reveals Your Strength

Surrender is not defeat - it is the ultimate strength. It says, "I trust the whole more than I trust the part." When you release control, life begins to support you in unexpected and miraculous ways.

Let Life Surprise You

The mind clings to plans, but the heart thrives in openness. When you stop predicting and controlling, you make space for wonder. Let each day unfold with curiosity, and life becomes a gift.

No One Can Give You What You Already Are

Love, peace, worth - they cannot be given to you by the world, because they are your nature. Stop seeking from others what can only be discovered within. You are already whole.

Choose Presence Over Perfection

Trying to be perfect keeps you trapped in the future. Presence brings you home. Be here, now, imperfect and real. It is in your presence - not your perfection - that transformation begins.

You Belong to This Moment

You are not an outsider to life. You are life itself, appearing as a human being. You belong here, now, exactly as you are. This moment is your rightful place. Enter it fully.

See with the Eyes of the Heart

The intellect may judge and divide, but the heart sees truth through love. When you look at others with the heart's wisdom, you see not their flaws but their essence. Let love become your lens.

The More You Let Go, the Lighter You Become

Each attachment weighs on the soul. When you release the need to possess, control, or be right, you rise into lightness. Letting go is not loss - it is liberation.

Peace Is the Ground of All Being

Beneath every thought, every emotion, every event, peace remains. It is the ever-present background of existence. When you stop clinging to the foreground, peace reveals itself.

Your True Nature Is Beyond Words

Language can point, but it cannot contain what you are. You are not a name, a label, or a description. You are the ineffable, infinite presence behind every word.

Be still and know.

You Are Never Alone

Even in silence, even in solitude, you are held
by life. The same essence that breathes stars
into being lives in you. Separation is illusion
- oneness is the truth. Feel the support
of the whole.

Don't Rush the Unfolding

A flower blooms in its own time. So do you. Awakening cannot be forced. Trust the pace of your becoming. You are not late, not behind, only in process.

Forgiveness Is Freedom

To forgive is not to condone - it is to release the burden you carry. What you refuse to forgive, you bind yourself to. Let go, not for them, but for your own peace.

You Are the Sky, Not the Weather

Storms may pass through, but they do not define the sky. You are the vast awareness in which all emotions arise and dissolve. Identify not with the storm, but with the spaciousness.

Nothing Is Outside the One

There is no true division in existence. All that you see, love, fear, or resist is part of the same whole. Unity does not exclude - it embraces all. Live from this inclusive vision.

Trust the Silence Between Thoughts

The gap between thoughts is not empty - it is full of presence. In those still moments, your true nature shines through. Rest there. The silence is not absence - it is the presence you seek.

Stay Open in the Unknown

The unknown can feel unsettling, but it is also alive with possibility. When you stay open, even without answers, you make space for wonder. Growth often hides where clarity hasn't yet arrived.

There Is No Spiritual Hierarchy

No one is more awakened than another. All beings are different expressions of the same infinite Self. The idea of spiritual levels belongs to the mind. The truth is beyond comparison - it is equal in all.

Let Awareness Include Everything

Don't push anything away. Let every thought, every feeling, every sensation be included in awareness. Inclusion is integration, and integration is healing. Everything belongs in the light of your presence.

Patience Is Trust in Time

To be patient is to trust the unfolding of life's rhythm. When you stop rushing, you begin to walk in harmony with the eternal. Patience is not waiting - it is resting in divine timing.

The Mind Cannot Grasp the Infinite

The infinite cannot be held by thought. It can only be surrendered to. Let the mind relax in not-knowing and allow the heart to feel what the intellect cannot comprehend. Truth is not understood - it is known.

Be Gentle with Yourself

Awakening is not a race, and healing is not a contest. Be kind to the parts of you that still struggle. Gentleness softens the ego's grip and invites the soul forward. You grow best in warmth.

Nothing Can Diminish the Self

No mistake, no trauma, no failure has ever touched your true nature. The Self is untouched, whole, and radiant. Like the sun behind the clouds, your essence shines no matter what passes before it.

Return Everything
to Love

Whatever arises - joy, pain, anger, fear - return it to love. Love is not only an emotion, but the nature of being. Bring all things home to the heart, and they are transformed.

Your Presence Is Enough

You don't need to perform, explain, or prove yourself. Your simple, sincere presence is the greatest offering you can make. Just be and let your being be a blessing to the world.

Nothing Real Can Be Lost

What is real in you can never be taken. If something disappears, it was never truly yours. Let the unreal fall away, and trust that what remains is what matters.

Awareness Is Your True Identity

You are not your name, your job, or your story. You are the timeless presence in which all these things arise. Rest in that knowing, and the roles you play no longer bind you - they serve you.

Let Love Be Your First Response

Before reaction, before defense, choose love. It's not always easy, but it is always possible. Love clears the path, disarms fear, and softens the hardened places within and around you.

Clarity Comes with Quiet

The answers you seek often lie beneath the surface noise. When the mind grows still, clarity emerges like the sun behind clouds. Don't chase clarity - invite it with silence.

You Are Carried by the Same Source as the Stars

The same force that spins galaxies also beats your heart. You are not separate from this intelligence - you are an expression of it. Trust that you are held, supported, and guided.

Suffering Lessens with Acceptance

The pain may still be there, but suffering is optional. When you stop fighting what is, you stop adding resistance to reality. Acceptance is not resignation - it is peace in action.

You Don't Need to Be Fixed

You are not broken. You may have forgotten, but nothing essential is missing. Growth is not about becoming better but remembering who you are beneath the conditioning.

Surrender Is a Returning

Surrender is not giving up - it is coming home. When you surrender, you return to the ground of your being, where nothing is lacking. From this space, wisdom and strength flow.

Listen to the Quiet Voice Within

Amid the noise of the world and the mind, there is a quiet voice always speaking. It does not shout. It whispers truth with gentle certainty. Trust that voice - it is your compass.

What You Judge, You Cannot See Clearly

Judgment clouds vision. When you release judgment, your perception clears. You begin to see people, situations, and yourself as they are, not as the mind wants them to be.

You Are the Answer You've Been Waiting For

The fulfillment you seek is not elsewhere - it is in you. Every path, every longing, every question leads back to your own being. You are the source and the solution. Look within, and you will find it.

Peace Begins Where Resistance Ends

The moment you stop resisting what is, a doorway opens. Peace does not need to be created - only uncovered. Let everything be as it is, and peace will meet you there.

The Soul Thrives on Simplicity

Simplicity nourishes the spirit. The quieter your life becomes, the more clearly you hear the call of the soul. Strip away the unnecessary, and what remains is sacred.

You Were Never Separate

The feeling of separation is the root illusion. In truth, you have always been one with all that is. This realization doesn't need effort - only recognition. You were never apart.

Let Your Breath Lead You Home

Your breath is a direct line to presence. It's always with you, always now. When the mind wanders, return to the breath. Let it guide you gently back to the stillness within.

Truth Needs No Defense

The truth does not argue or defend itself. It stands quietly, radiant and unshaken. When you live from truth, there is no need to convince. Your presence becomes your message.

Everything Is Teaching You

Every challenge, every joy, every ordinary moment is a teacher in disguise. Nothing is wasted. Life itself is the curriculum. Meet each experience with openness, and you will grow.

Be Where Your Feet Are

The mind can run far into the past or future, but your feet are always here. Let them remind you: this is the only place where life happens. Be here, fully, grateful.

Your Light Is Not Meant to Be Hidden

There is a radiance in you that wants to shine. Not for approval, but as a natural expression of being. Don't dim yourself. Let your light be a blessing to the world.

Awakening Is Remembering, Not Becoming

You do not need to turn into something else - you need only remember what you are. Under every layer of conditioning lies the untouched truth. You are already that.

The Self Is Silent, Still, and Free

Your essence does not move, change, or strive. It is silent, still, and utterly free. When you rest in the Self, the noise of the world loses its grip, and only freedom remains.

The Now Is Always Enough

This moment is not lacking. It holds everything needed for peace, joy, and clarity. The mind may chase another time, but the heart knows: the fullness of life is always now.

Freedom Arises in Letting Be

Freedom doesn't always come from doing, but from letting be. When you stop trying to fix, force, or flee, you find space. In this space, the Self is free to shine.

You Are the Witness, Not the Wave

Emotions rise and fall like waves. But you are the ocean - the vast, unchanging witness of them all. Return to the witness and find peace beneath the motion.

Love Is Who You Are

You do not need to search for love - it is your very being. When all pretenses fall away, what remains is love, quiet and true. Be what you are, and love flows effortlessly.

Each Moment Is a Doorway

No moment is wasted. Every breath, every encounter, every silence is a doorway to presence. Step through the mundane and discover the miraculous waiting there.

Let Truth Undo You

Truth is not always comfortable, but it is always liberating. Let it undo false identities and open you to deeper being. What falls away was never truly you.

Silence Holds
Every Answer

When the questions grow loud, let silence speak. It holds the answers not in words, but in presence. Trust the still voice - it arises from your deepest Self.

You Are Held by the Infinite

Even when you feel lost or alone, the infinite holds you. You are never truly separate. You exist within the embrace of Being itself, safe and eternal.

Being Is the Greatest Doing

There is no higher act than to simply be fully present. Presence changes everything - it heals, reveals, and restores. Before you act, pause, and be. From being, right action flows.

Awareness Knows No Boundaries

Awareness is not confined to your body or your thoughts. It is spacious, boundless, and free. When you recognize yourself as awareness, you are no longer limited - you are limitless.

The Divine Is Always Present

You do not need to go far or climb high to reach the Divine. It is here - in your breath, your heartbeat, your stillness. The sacred is woven into the fabric of every moment.

Let Yourself Be Moved by Wonder

Wonder cracks open the shell of certainty. Let yourself be awed by a leaf, a smile, a sunrise. Wonder reawakens your heart to the mystery of being.

Everything Is Made of Light

At the most fundamental level, all things are vibrations of the same essence - light. This is not metaphor but truth. See the light in yourself and in others, and the illusion of difference fades.

Don't Be Afraid of Emptiness

Emptiness is not a void but a vastness. In it is peace, presence, and pure potential. Let the empty spaces expand - they are not hollow, but holy.

Let the Heart Be Your Guide

The mind may plan, but the heart knows. When you let the heart lead, you walk in truth. It may be quieter than thought, but its guidance is always loving, always true.

You Are the Open Sky

Clouds come and go - moods, events, thoughts. But the sky remains. You are the openness in which all things arise and pass. Rest in the sky, not the storm.

The Present Moment Is a Portal

You do not enter truth through the future. You enter it through the now. Each moment is a portal to the eternal. Step in through presence and find the infinite waiting.

There Is Grace in Every Experience

Even in pain, grace is present. It may not be obvious, but it is there, inviting you deeper into compassion, surrender, and truth. Trust that every experience holds something sacred.

You Are the Space Between Thoughts

You are not your thinking. You are the stillness in which thoughts appear and disappear. Rest in the space between, and know your true self.

Life Is Happening for You, Not to You

Every moment is perfectly tailored for your awakening. Life is not against you - it is shaping you, revealing you, and leading you back to your Self.

The Heart Understands What Words Cannot

There are truths that no explanation can contain. The heart knows them without needing proof. When the mind falls silent, the heart speaks - listen with your whole being.

You Are Not
Your Thoughts

Thoughts arise and fall, but you remain. You are the awareness that watches, not the noise that comes and goes. The less you identify with thought, the more peace you uncover.

Presence Is the Purest Prayer

You don't need special words or rituals
to commune with the Divine. Your full
presence is enough. When you are truly here,
even in silence, you are in prayer.

Let the Mystery Be Sacred

Not everything must be solved or explained. Some things are meant to be met with reverence, not reason. The mystery is not a problem - it is a portal.

You Are the Still Point in the Turning World

While everything moves and changes, there is a still point within you that remains. Return to it. Let that quiet center become your anchor, no matter the storm.

Nothing Outside Can Complete You

Wholeness is not found in possessions, achievements, or relationships. It is remembered within. You are already complete. What you long for is your own presence.

Let the Mind Bow
to the Heart

The mind serves beautifully when led by the heart. Let your thoughts follow love, not fear. When the heart leads, clarity and compassion walk hand in hand.

There Is Wisdom in Surrender

Surrender is not giving up; it is opening up. When you stop trying to control everything, wisdom flows in. Let life be your teacher and surrender be your guide.

Be at Home in the Unknown

You don't need all the answers to feel safe. Make peace with mystery. Let the unknown become a place of trust, not fear. Growth begins where certainty ends.

Everything You Need Is Already Here

You are not lacking. The tools, insights, and love you need are already present - within or around you. Slow down. Look again. The abundance of now awaits your noticing.

Awareness Is Your Eternal Home

Before the body, before the mind, there is awareness. It was never born and never dies. To rest in awareness is to come home to yourself, beyond all change.

Allow, and the Way Appears

Struggle clouds clarity. But when you allow what is, the path becomes visible. Surrender reveals the next step - not always the one you expected, but always the one you need.

The World Reflects Your Inner State

Your perceptions shape your experience. When you shift within, the world shifts without. Peace, love, and clarity are not found in changing the world, but in changing how you see it.

Let Every Breath Be a Benediction

Each breath is a blessing - an affirmation of life, a return to now. When you breathe consciously, you bless the body, the mind, and the moment. Let your breath be your prayer.

You Are Not Here to Fix Yourself

You are not broken. The journey is not about correction but revelation. Peel back what is false, and your wholeness shines through. You are already enough.

Compassion Is the Natural Language of the Soul

When you see with the soul's eyes, judgment falls away. What remains is compassion - a soft, steady love for all beings, including yourself. Let this be your language.

Rest in the Presence of What Is

You do not need to escape the moment to find peace. Peace lives inside the moment. Rest with what is, without needing to alter or escape, and presence will meet you.

The Truth Is Always Simple

Complexity confuses; truth clarifies. Real wisdom is simple, direct, and quietly powerful. Trust what is simple - it often carries the deepest truth.

Grace Moves Quietly

You may not see it, but grace is always working - softening, guiding, healing. Trust its quiet movements. When you look back, you'll see it was there all along.

You Are the Answer to Your Deepest Question

The longing, the searching, the seeking - all point back to you. The answer is not found in the future or the world. The answer is your own presence, discovered in stillness.

Let Awareness
Be Your Anchor

When emotions pull and thoughts swirl, return to awareness. It is the steady ground beneath the changing tides. In awareness, you find peace not because life is calm, but because you are.

Joy Is Not in Things, but in Being

The deepest joy arises not from possessions or praise, but from presence. When you rest fully in being, joy arises on its own, simple and unconditional.

Every Heartbeat Is a Reminder of Now

Let your heartbeat remind you - you are alive, here, now. Each pulse is life loving you into existence. Come back to the rhythm of now and let it center you.

The Soul Speaks Through Silence

Silence is not empty; it is full of knowing. When you stop filling every space with words and distractions, your soul has room to speak. Listen in the quiet.

You Are the Witness of Time

Time moves, but you are the stillness in which it appears. The past is memory, the future imagination - only this awareness is real. Be the witness, and time loses its hold.

You Belong to the Whole

You are not separate. You are not other. You belong to this earth, this sky, this moment. Everything that is, includes you. Rest in your belonging.

Let Peace Be Your Natural State

You don't need to earn peace - it is your default state of being. Beneath every worry, fear, or distraction lies peace, waiting. Return to it, not through striving, but by stopping.

Be Gentle with the Process

Awakening is not a straight line. Some days will feel clear, others clouded. Be gentle. Trust the ebb and flow. The path is unfolding perfectly, even when you cannot see it.

There Is Room for All of You

You do not need to suppress or exile any part of yourself. There is room in awareness for your joy, sorrow, confusion, and clarity. Let all be seen, and all will soften.

Truth Feels Like Home

You know truth not because it convinces,
but because it resonates. It feels like a return.
When you find it, there is no fanfare - only a
quiet sense of homecoming.

Let Your Life Be Your Practice

You don't need to escape to a cave or climb a mountain. Every interaction, every task, every breath is your path. Life is the practice. Live it mindfully, and the sacred is revealed.

What You Resist, Stays

Resistance is glue. Whatever you fight, you bind too. But when you allow what is, it loses power over you. Freedom begins with letting things be.

Truth Is Not Fragile

Truth does not need defense. It does not crumble under scrutiny. It is strong, resilient, and patient. Trust that truth will stand even when everything else falls away.

Presence Needs No Improvement

Presence doesn't require fixing, achieving, or adjusting. It simply is. Rest in presence, and discover the peace that was always here, waiting quietly behind the noise.

The Self Cannot Be Touched by Thought

Thought can describe but never define you. You are not what you think - you are the one who knows thought. That knowing is untouched, still, and ever free.

Life Is Not a Problem to Be Solved

You are not here to figure everything out. You are here to live, to love, to be. The mind will seek answers. The heart knows it is already whole.

Choose Stillness Over Striving

In a world that values motion, choose stillness. In stillness, insight arises. In stillness, you remember your true nature. Be still - and know.

You Are Always Connected

Even when you feel alone, the thread of being connects you to all. The separation is only in thought. The truth is unity - always.

Rest Is a Revolutionary Act

To rest is to resist the speed of the world and return to your center. Rest renews the soul, heals the body, and reveals the sacred. Make space to rest - and remember.

There Is Nowhere
to Get To

The destination you long for is not
elsewhere. It is here, now, in this very breath.
Stop chasing. Begin noticing. You have
already arrived.

Let This Moment Be Enough

You don't need to add or subtract anything. This moment, as it is, is enough. Be here. Be open. Let the Now be all that it is - nothing more, nothing less.

You Are Not the Doer

Life flows through you like wind through the trees. The idea that you are in control is only a thought. Relax into being done through you and find peace in surrender.

The Soul Moves at the Speed of Trust

You cannot rush awakening. The soul unfolds in trust, not in force. Walk slowly, breathe deeply, and let the journey guide you in its own time.

There Is Power in Non-Reaction

To pause before responding is to reclaim your power. In that still point, you become free from reactivity. From that space, true wisdom arises.

Light Cannot Be Touched by Darkness

Darkness is only the absence of light. It has no force of its own. When light enters, darkness disappears. Be the light, and do not fear the shadow.

The Present Moment Has No Opposite

Past and future are thought forms. Only the present is real. Rest in what is now, and you will touch the eternal.

Grace Often Wears Disguise

Grace may not look like what you expect. It may come as loss, silence, or delay. Trust it anyway. Grace is always moving for your highest good.

You Were Never Lost

Even in confusion, you were held. Even in fear, you were loved. You cannot fall out of the whole. You were never lost - only learning.

The Sacred Lives in the Ordinary

You don't need mountaintops to find the holy. It's in the dishes, the laughter, the quiet afternoons. See the ordinary clearly, and you'll find the Divine.

Presence Turns Every Act into a Blessing

It's not what you do, but the awareness you bring to it. When done with presence, even the smallest gesture becomes a sacred offering.

The Truth of Who You Are Is Always Intact

No matter what you've been through, the truth of your being remains whole. Your essence is never damaged. It simply waits to be remembered, like the sky behind the clouds.

Allow Yourself to Be Fully Human

You are divine, yes, but also wonderfully human. Let your joy, your grief, your flaws and strengths be part of your walk. Nothing needs to be denied - everything is sacred.

The Eternal Is Found in the Ordinary

You don't need to seek the infinite in far-off temples. It lives in the steam of your tea, the sound of your breath, the softness of your gaze. Eternity is here.

Love Needs
No Justification

You don't need a reason to love. Love flows
because it is your nature. Let it move without
condition, agenda, or reward.
Let it be as it is - free.

Surrender Is the Path of the Brave

It takes great courage to let go. To surrender is not weakness - it is the strength to trust the unknown, to release control, and to bow to something greater than thought.

You Are Already What You Seek

Every spiritual search ends at home – from here to here. What you seek - peace, love, unity - is already within you. When the seeking stops, what you truly are is revealed.

Let What Wants to Fall, Fall

Don't cling to what is passing. If something is meant to leave, let it go with grace. What remains is truer. What comes next is more aligned.

You Can Begin Again at Any Moment

The past does not define you. Each breath offers renewal. Begin again - not from the old story, but from presence. Life always invites a fresh start.

The Mind Wants to Grasp, the Soul Wants to Trust

The mind demands understanding, the soul rests in mystery. You don't need to know everything. You only need to trust the unfolding.

All Is Well, Even When It Seems Otherwise

Beneath the chaos, there is order. Beneath the pain, love is still present. You may not see the whole picture, but trust: all is truly well.

The Path Is Made
by Walking

You don't need to have it all figured out.
Just take the next step. With each step in
presence, the path becomes clear. The way is
made by walking.

Stillness Is the Greatest Teacher

Beneath every answer you seek lies stillness.
It teaches not with words, but with presence.
Enter the stillness and discover the truth
beyond thought.

Your Nature Is Spacious

You are not the noise, the form, the drama.
You are the space in which all arises. Return
again and again to this spacious awareness -
and be free.

Let the Divine Work Through You

You are not separate from the Source. Let yourself be a channel - empty, open, available. The more you let go, the more grace can move through you.

The Now Is Untouched by Story

Stories live in the mind, but now lives in the body, in awareness. Drop the narrative. Enter the Now. It is always fresh, always new, always free.

Resistance Creates Suffering

Pain is part of life, but suffering arises when we resist what is. Let go of the fight. Let it be. Peace lives in the space where resistance ends.

There Is a Light That Never Goes Out

No matter how dark the night is, there is a light within you that never dims. Return to it. Trust it. It is your truth, and it is eternal.

Let Simplicity Be Your Compass

The truth is always simple. Complexity is the language of the mind. Let simplicity guide your decisions, your relationships, your path - it will not lead you astray.

You Are the Calm in the Center

Life may whirl around you, but you are not the storm. You are the calm eye in the center. Return to this still point and let it hold you.

Everything Belongs

Nothing needs to be excluded. Every part of
you, every moment of your life, has a place.
When you welcome everything, you discover
the oneness in all.

Your Soul Remembers What the Mind Forgets

Beyond the grasp of thought, your soul carries timeless wisdom. In moments of stillness or awe, you remember who you are - not through thought, but through being.

Even Sorrow Can Be a Sacred Door

Do not fear sorrow. Let it open you, soften you, deepen you. Within sorrow lives the seed of compassion, the invitation to love more truly.

You Are Already Held

Before you seek, you are held. Before you pray, you are heard. The universe is not indifferent - it is love itself, wrapping itself around you.

Be Willing to Be Empty

Emptiness is not the absence of meaning,
but the space in which meaning appears. Be
willing to be empty, and the truth will
fill you.

The Still Point Within Is Always Accessible

No matter the chaos, you can return to the still point within. It is your sanctuary. Close your eyes, breathe, and feel it - always waiting, always present.

You Are the Dreamer, Not the Dream

This life is a play of forms, sensations, and identities. You are not the content of the dream - you are the one who sees it. Wake up to your witnessing.

Let Each Act Be an Offering

It is not what you do but how you do it. Let each act - washing dishes, speaking, walking - be done in love. This turns your whole life into worship.

You Are Never Outside the Divine

You may feel separate, but the Divine never abandons. Like waves on the ocean, you rise and fall in it. You are made of it, and you are never apart.

Awareness Is Not in the Body, the Body Is in Awareness

Your awareness is not limited to your form. It is vast and borderless. The body moves in it, appears in it - but you are the boundless space itself.

Rest Is a Form of Trust

To rest is to say: I trust. I trust life to continue without my effort. I trust my worth beyond productivity. Rest is not withdrawal - it is surrender to what is.

Clarity Comes from Stillness, Not Striving

When the waters of the mind settle, clarity appears on its own. You do not have to push for answers. Rest in stillness, and truth will find you.

The Infinite Wears a Human Face

Each person you meet is the face of the infinite. Look beyond the mask, and you will see yourself. Every encounter is a mirror.

Let Life Love You

Stop holding yourself apart from the goodness of life. Let it reach you. Let it bless you. The love you seek is already pouring in.

Inner Peace Is a Choice, Not a Condition

Peace does not depend on the world being calm. It arises when you choose not to be disturbed within. Make that choice - and keep making it.

You Are Not Here to Fix the World

The world does not need fixing - it needs your presence. Show up fully. Love deeply. Act with clarity. That is enough.

Trust the Intelligence of the Whole

You do not have to figure everything out.
Life is intelligent. It unfolds with a wisdom
far beyond thought. Trust the process.

Even in Emptiness, You Are Full

When all else is stripped away, what remains is fullness. A presence, vast and alive, fills the silence. This is your true nature.

Forgiveness Frees the One Who Forgives

Forgiveness is not about condoning - it is about releasing. It cuts the chains and sets you free. Let it be an act of liberation.

The Universe Moves at the Speed of Love

Love is not slow or fast - it is timeless. Trust its rhythm. Let it guide your actions. What moves with love, moves in harmony.

You Are the Space Where Everything Happens

Thoughts, emotions, experiences - all arise in you. But you are not them. You are the space in which they come and go. Stay as that and be free.

The Light You Seek Is Already Shining

You do not need to light a new flame - only to remove the coverings. Beneath fear, beneath thought, your light is shining. Be still and know it.

Oneness Does Not Exclude Differences

Unity is not sameness. The many are expressions of the One. Celebrate diversity and let it remind you of the deep harmony behind all forms.

The Soul Lives in the Present Tense

The soul is not concerned with what was or what might be. It knows only now. To live from the soul, drop into the immediacy of this moment.

You Are Not the Story, but the Silent Reader

The story of your life is not who you are. You are the awareness reading it. Let the story unfold, but rest in the reader - unchanging and free.

Everything You Lose Reveals What Cannot Be Lost

Loss is not the end - it is a clearing. It reveals what is eternal, what no time or change can touch. Let loss show you your indestructible Self.

The Depth of Being Is Wordless

Words can guide, but the truth lies deeper.
Go beyond the concepts. Let yourself
fall into the silent depth where all words
dissolve, and only knowing remains.

The Most Powerful Presence Is Gentle

True power does not force. It does not dominate. It simply is - quiet, radiant, unshakable. Let gentleness be your strength.

Nothing Real Can Be Threatened

What is real in you cannot be harmed.
Not by loss, not by time, not by death. It is
beyond all change. Rest in that,
and fear fades.

Let Awareness Flow into Every Corner

Shine awareness on the hidden places. Not to fix, but to see. The light of awareness is healing in itself. Wherever it touches, it brings clarity.

You Belong to the Infinite, and It Belongs to You

You are not a visitor here. You are the universe remembering itself. You belong - and in your belonging, the whole becomes conscious of itself.

The Sacred Is Closer Than Your Breath

You don't need to seek far and wide. The sacred is here, in your next breath, your next blink, the stillness behind your eyes. Stay close to what is already close.

Peace Arises When You Stop Arguing with Reality

Suffering begins with resistance. When you stop the internal fight and allow what is, peace dawns naturally, quietly, like a forgotten friend.

What You Truly Are Cannot Be Found, Only Realized

You cannot seek what you already are. All paths, all teachings, point you back to the one looking. Stop seeking. Start being.

Let the Mystery Hold You

You don't need to understand everything. Some things are meant to be lived, not solved. Let the mystery be your companion - not your enemy.

The Deepest Knowing Is Wordless Recognition

Some truths cannot be spoken. They shine in
the eyes, in presence, in stillness. When you
meet them, you just know -
and that is enough.

You Are the Presence Behind the Personality

Your name, your story, your role -
all come and go. But what remains?
Presence. Unchanging. Awake.
That is what you truly are.

There Is No Path to Oneness, Only the Realization There Was Never Separation

Oneness isn't reached - it's revealed. When the illusion of separation dissolves, what's left is what always was: wholeness.

Don't Hurry
the Unfolding

Each petal of your being opens in its time.
You are not behind. You are not late. Trust
the pace of your blooming.

Allow Stillness
to Soften You

Stillness is not stagnation. It is depth. It is surrender. It is where the sharp edges of the self melt into something vast and tender.

The Divine Recognizes Itself in You

When you look with love, speak from truth, act from presence - the Divine sees itself in your form. You are not apart from it. You are its revelation.

Let Silence Teach You What Words Cannot

There is a depth that no teaching can reach, but silence knows the way. In silence, truth ripens. In silence, you remember without needing to be told.

Awareness Is Always Unmoved

Storms may shake the sky, but the sky remains unchanged. You are the sky of awareness - unmoved, untouched by passing weather. Rest in your vastness.

Everything You Long For Is Already Within

The love, the peace, the wholeness - they are not found out there. They arise when you turn inward and sit quietly with what already is.

Your Breath Is the Bridge Between Form and Spirit

With each inhale, you are filled with the sacred. With each exhale, you release the illusion. The breath carries you back to truth, again and again.

Grace Comes When You Stop Grasping

You cannot force grace. It appears when you stop clutching, when you surrender, when you are willing to receive without demand.

Let Yourself Be Loved by the Moment

Let the moment cradle you. Let the wind, the stillness, the sound, the space - touch you. When you let yourself be loved, you remember that you always were.

The Deepest Truths
Are Simple

The mind seeks complexity, but the soul whispers simplicity: I am. You are. This is. Let go of more, and you will find everything.

No Experience Can Add to Who You Are

You are not improved by your experiences -
you are revealed. Let every moment uncover,
not define, the light that already shines
in you.

Even Darkness Is Held by the Light

There is no place where the light does not reach. Even your darkest moments are known, held, enfolded in something luminous. Trust that the light has never left you.

Let Go Into the Infinite

You do not fall when you let go. You rise into
freedom, to clarity, into the embrace of what
always was. Let go and let the Infinite
catch you.

The More You Let Go, the More You Become

Shedding is not loss - it is revelation. The more you release, the more your true nature shines. Let yourself be uncovered, not diminished.

Presence Is the Most Healing Force

No technique, no doctrine, no effort surpasses presence. When you are fully here, you touch the eternal - and in that touch, healing begins.

Time Is the Canvas, You Are the Painter

You are not bound by the past or future. They are colors on the canvas, but your awareness holds the brush. Create wisely, from presence.

Stillness Is Not an Absence - It Is Fullness

True stillness brims with aliveness. It is not the absence of motion, but the presence of being. Enter it, and you meet your boundless self.

Don't Just Witness Life - Be Life

There is no distance between you and what is. You are not merely a watcher - you are the breath, the bird, the breeze. You are Life expressing itself.

The Quietest Voice Is Often the Truest

Truth does not shout. It whispers. It stirs gently in the heart. Make space to hear it, and you'll find it was speaking all along.

Your Essence Is Not an Idea

No thought, no concept can define what you are. You are not your beliefs - you are the awareness in which they arise and dissolve. Go deeper than ideas.

The Sacred Cannot Be Found - Only Recognized

Nothing needs to be added for life to be sacred. It already is. Open your eyes. Let reverence arise in the ordinary.
That is awakening.

The Soul Speaks Through Simplicity

The soul speaks not in complexity, but in quiet clarity. A touch, a breath, a sunset - these are its language. Listen for its gentle tone.

The Divine Is Always Whispering "Yes"

To your being, your breath, your becoming - the Divine says yes. Let yourself feel that yes in the core of your being. Let it carry you home.

You Are the Holy Flame, Not Just the Candle

The candle burns out, the flame continues. You are not the form that flickers - you are the eternal flame, untouched by the winds of change.

Let the Sacred Saturate the Ordinary

The cup, the floor, the silence between words - each is lit with divinity. See with the eyes of reverence, and the mundane becomes miraculous.

You Are the Prayer Answering Itself

The longing you feel is the Divine reaching for you as you reach for It. You and the Beloved are not separate. You are the call, the echo, and the fulfillment.

Be the Silence That Holds the Sound

Do not chase the notes. Be the silence that allows them. In that sacred holding, all things arise and return - untouched, whole.

Love Is Not an Emotion, but a State of Being

Love is not something you feel for another. It is what you are when all pretense drops. Let yourself return to that radiant center.

The Divine Is Closer Than Thought

Thought creates distance. But the Divine is not a concept to be reached - it is the ground you stand on, the breath you forget to notice. Simply be.

You Are the Stillness Beneath All Motion

Waves rise and fall, but the ocean is still. In the same way, be the stillness beneath your life's rising and falling. You are vast. You are peace.

All That Is Sacred Welcomes You

You do not need to be better, purer, or more enlightened to belong. The sacred welcomes you as you are, because you are already That.

Let the Light Within Lead You Home

The world will offer many directions, but only the light within knows the way. Follow its warmth. It never falters.

There Is No End to Awakening

Enlightenment is not a peak, but a pathless unfolding. It is a lifelong deepening, a continuous softening into what already is.

Enter the Heart
of Silence

Beyond sound, beyond thought, there is
a silence not of emptiness but of sacred
fullness. In this silence, the Self is known not
as concept, but as radiance.

The Divine Breathes Through You

Every breath is a miracle. The air that enters you is not separate from the One that gives it. Let yourself be breathed - by love, by life, by grace.

You Are the Temple and the Light Within

No need to seek holy ground - it is you. The sacred is not outside. You are both the vessel and the flame. Honor yourself with reverence.

Every Moment Is a Doorway to the Infinite

You need not wait for the perfect condition. Right now, in this ordinary moment, the Infinite invites you in. Step through, gently.

Let the Beloved Move Through Your Hands

Whatever you touch, touch with love. Let your hands become instruments of blessing, your gestures offerings of the Sacred made visible.

The Divine Wears Your Face

You are not just made in the image of God -
you are God remembering itself as you. Your
eyes are the windows through which love
sees the world.

Surrender Is the Highest Prayer

You need not find the right words. To surrender fully is to pray with your whole being. It says: Thy will, not mine. And in that, you are held.

Holiness Is Not Perfection - It Is Presence

You do not need to be flawless to be holy.
Holiness is found in the undivided now,
where nothing is hidden, and all is allowed.

Be the Still Flame
in the Storm

Even as the winds howl and waves crash,
remain as the flame that does not waver. This
is not resistance - it is remembrance of your
eternal Self.

The Sacred Knows Your Name

Before you ask, you are known. Before you strive, you are loved. The Sacred does not forget you - it sings your name in silence, always.

The Light You Carry Illuminates All Paths

You may not always see it, but your very being shines. You carry a light that does not diminish with time or hardship. Walk as though you are lit from within - because you are.

Let Grace Have Its Way with You

Stop shaping the river. Let it shape you.
Grace flows when you yield, when you trust
the unseen hands that guide your unfolding.

Even the Shadows Serve the Light

Darkness is not the enemy - it is the canvas on which light is seen. Do not fear your shadow; meet it with love, and it too becomes sacred.

You Are Already Inside the Heart of God

There is no distance to travel. No door to unlock. You are already home. What keeps you from feeling it is only the veil of forgetting.

All That You Are Is Welcome Here

Bring your doubts, your wounds, your unfinished places. The Holy does not demand perfection. It asks only for your presence - honest and whole.

Rest in the Awareness That Knows No Edges

Close your eyes and sense into that which has no boundary, no beginning or end. That is you - not the body, not the story, but the spacious knowing.

The Most Profound Teachings Are Wordless

Let the wind teach you. Let the sky, the stars, the stillness between your heartbeats be your teacher. They speak in truth beyond language.

Let the Sacred Touch You Where You Think You're Broken

You are not broken, only breaking open. Let the Divine meet you in those tender cracks. That is where the light enters, and where healing begins.

This Moment Is the Gate to Eternity

Not tomorrow. Not after the next awakening. This moment, right now, holds the whole of God. Step into it fully, and the veil dissolves.

You Are the Song the Universe Is Singing

You are not separate from the Source - you are its expression. Like a note in a vast symphony, your presence makes the whole more complete.

The Sacred Rests in What You Allow

Not in what you force, fix, or strive to change. The Sacred is found in your yes - in your willingness to be with life exactly as it is.

Your Soul Has Never Forgotten the Way

Even when you feel lost, even when doubt clouds your mind - your soul knows. It remembers the path, the Source, the truth. Let it lead.

You Are Held by What You Cannot Name

There is a Love too vast to describe, too quiet to demand your attention. But it holds you now, as it always has. Be still and know.

Trust What You Know in the Quiet

Beneath noise, beneath reaction, there is a still knowing. Trust it. It comes not from fear, not from thought, but from the sacred depth within.

You Are Not Becoming, You Are Returning

This path is not about becoming someone new. It is a return to what you have always been. Remove what is false, and you remain.

The Divine Is Not a Destination, but a Presence

You do not arrive at the Divine - you notice it. In the pause, in the prayer, in the kindness unspoken. It is always here.

Let the Mystery Undress You

Let yourself be stripped of roles, beliefs, defenses. Stand bare before the Mystery - not to be judged, but to be revealed.

Nothing You Truly Are Can Be Threatened

The passing world may tremble, but your essence is unshakable. Let fear fall away in the face of this radiant truth.

Be the Sanctuary
You Seek

You are the temple. You are the refuge. What you long for in others, offer to yourself. Your presence is holy ground.

Love Is the Final Answer to Every Question

Not the sentimental kind, but the love that simply is. Let it dissolve the questions. Let it answer with presence, with peace, with truth.

The Sacred Is Always Whispering Your Name

In every breeze, every silence, every moment of stillness - the sacred calls you home. Listen. It has never stopped speaking to you.

Lay Down the Armor of the Self

You don't need to defend or prove. Beneath all layers of identity is a heart already enough. Let it be seen, uncovered, held.

Let the Eternal Breathe Through the Now

Every moment is infused with the Infinite.
Let yourself pause, open, receive. The eternal
is not later - it is this breath, now.

God Does Not Reside in the Future

Stop postponing your holiness. The Divine meets you in this very place, this very breath. Do not look forward. Look deeper.

You Are the Wellspring of What You Seek

You search for peace, joy, love - yet they arise from within you. You are the source and the witness. Drink from your own well.

Rest in the Unnameable

Beyond religion, beyond doctrine, beyond form is the vast silence of Being. Let go of names. What remains is sacred beyond words.

Nothing Is Missing in This Moment

What if nothing needed to change? What if now was complete, whole, enough? Let the striving fall away and meet the fullness already here.

The Divine Walks Barefoot With You

There is no distance between you and God. The sacred walks beside you - in your doubts, your laughter, your everyday steps. You are never alone.

Your Being Is the Answer to the World's Cry

Not your opinions, not your performance - your presence. Let your being be an anchor of peace. It changes the world more than you know.

Be as You Were Before the First Thought

Before mind arose, before memory and
name - you were. Return to that innocence.
It is not lost. It is simply waiting to
be remembered.

The Final Step Is No Step at All

You stand at the end of seeking - not because you've arrived, but because you've remembered: there is nowhere to go.

You are That.

You Are the Mirror in Which God Sees God

Look gently inward. What you behold is not personal, but universal. You are the eye through which Love witnesses itself.

Let the Veil Fall Without Fear

The veil was never real. Only a thin mist of forgetting. Let it fall. What remains is not loss, but the radiant truth that was always yours.

Return Everything to the Heart

The mind seeks to divide and define. The heart simply knows. Return everything - your questions, your grief, your joy - to the sanctuary of the heart.

You Were
Never Separate

This is the final knowing: the journey was a circle, not a line. You were never lost. You were always the ocean, dreaming of being a wave.

NOTES

About the Author

For a lifetime, EKL has been walking the long, winding, sometimes hilarious, sometimes humbling road toward understanding who we really are. That road from childhood poverty to philosophy, religion, quantum physics, heartbreak, and awakening has led to a book whose moment has truly arrived.

www.ingramcontent.com/pod-product-compliance
Lightning Source LLC
Chambersburg PA
CBHW040744120726
48005CB00012B/1058